The Fables of Maui and Momma Cat

CAMDEN PET

HOSPITAL

-1960-

15-6

Walter R. Hoge, DVM

Printed in the United States of America

ISBN 979-8-89114-264-0 (sc)
ISBN 979-8-89114-265-7 (hc)
ISBN 979-8-89114-266-4 (e)

Library of Congress Control Number: 2026901447

2026.01.28

MainSpring Books
5901 W. Century Blvd
Suite 750
Los Angeles, CA, US, 90045

www.mainspringbooks.com

Companion animals usually spend only a short time in our lives, yet they have the ability to offer unconditional love, companionship, and a sense of balance within the natural world as a benevolent, powerful, life-giving force known as Mother Nature. *"The heavens belong to the Lord, but the earth He has given to mankind"* (Psalm 115:16). This gives us stewardship—God entrusting the earth to humanity to care for, cultivate, and govern responsibly. It admonishes us to respect and cooperate with nature rather than dominate the planet.

In September 2001, my kids' mom, Sheryl, noticed a young kitten stalking a mourning dove in our backyard near the swimming pool. Mourning doves, native to North America, range from southern Canada and the United States down into Mexico and Central America. They are a widespread species, thriving in various environments including forests, agricultural areas, and suburban neighborhoods. They feed almost exclusively on seeds and grains—wild grasses, weeds, cultivated crops like wheat and corn, and even peanuts. They forage on the ground in areas with bare soil, occasionally consuming berries or small snails. They eat large quantities of seeds at once, storing food in a crop in their esophagus, and swallow grit to help grind the seeds for digestion.

Mourning dove nests are simple platforms of twigs, pine needles, and grass, often built in tree crotches or shrubs 5–25 feet high, though occasionally on the ground. The female lays two creamy-white eggs, and both parents incubate them for about 14 days, taking turns at the nest. They can have up to five or six broods a year. Their primary strategy for predator defense is nest site selection—choosing areas with natural cover and openness to reduce visibility of their flimsy nests. Their muted plumage provides excellent camouflage, allowing them to freeze in place. They also drink quickly to reduce vulnerability at watering spots, and their young hide in dense foliage or under porches, avoiding areas with signs of predators.

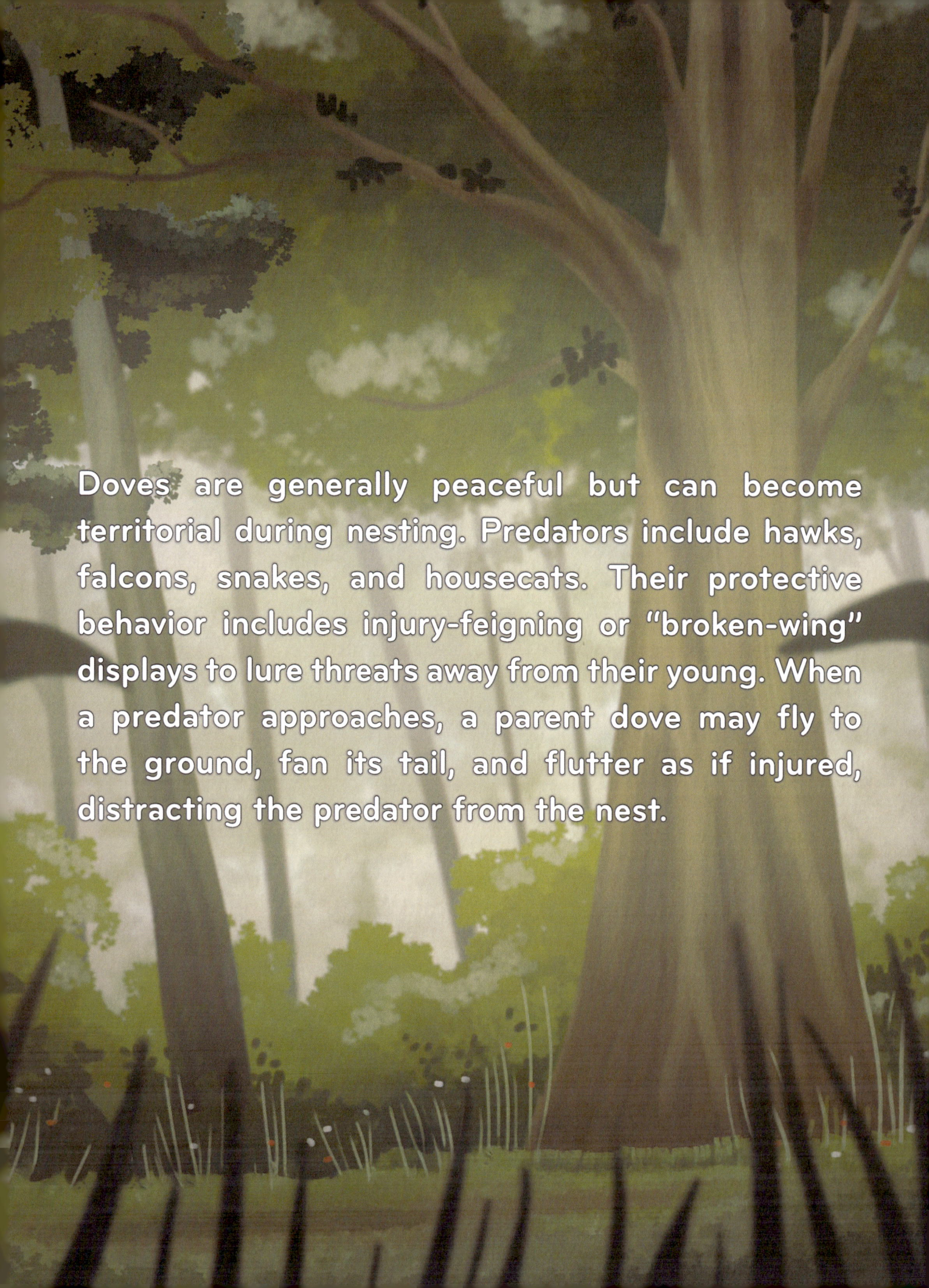

Doves are generally peaceful but can become territorial during nesting. Predators include hawks, falcons, snakes, and housecats. Their protective behavior includes injury-feigning or "broken-wing" displays to lure threats away from their young. When a predator approaches, a parent dove may fly to the ground, fan its tail, and flutter as if injured, distracting the predator from the nest.

The dove in our yard flew close to the kitten, landing in front of it and pecking at the ground as if searching for food. When the kitten prepared to pounce, the dove began performing the broken-wing display, always staying just out of reach. She repeated this until the kitten was far from the nest she had built among the open rafters above our hot tub and wooden deck. In that nest were two young squabs awaiting their next meal—a nutrient-dense substance called pigeon milk, produced in the crops of both parents.

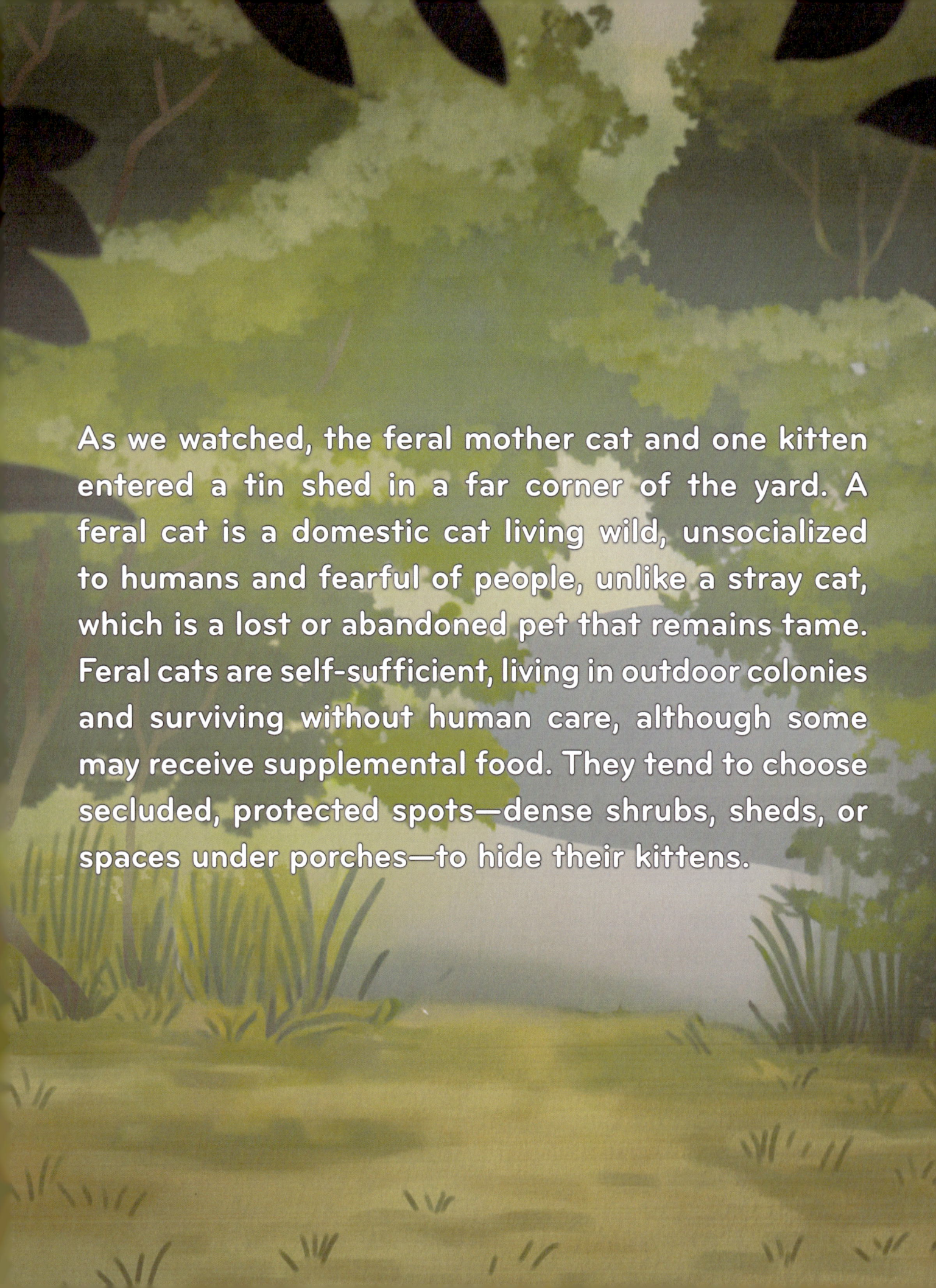

As we watched, the feral mother cat and one kitten entered a tin shed in a far corner of the yard. A feral cat is a domestic cat living wild, unsocialized to humans and fearful of people, unlike a stray cat, which is a lost or abandoned pet that remains tame. Feral cats are self-sufficient, living in outdoor colonies and surviving without human care, although some may receive supplemental food. They tend to choose secluded, protected spots—dense shrubs, sheds, or spaces under porches—to hide their kittens.

Taming feral kittens involves trapping them and keeping them in a confined, safe space such as a bathroom or kennel. Socialization uses positive reinforcement—food, treats, gentle handling, and calm voices. A tame adult cat can also model desirable behavior. Patience is essential; taming may take weeks or months, especially for older kittens. The most successful socialization window is between 2 and 8 weeks old, ideally 6 to 10 weeks.

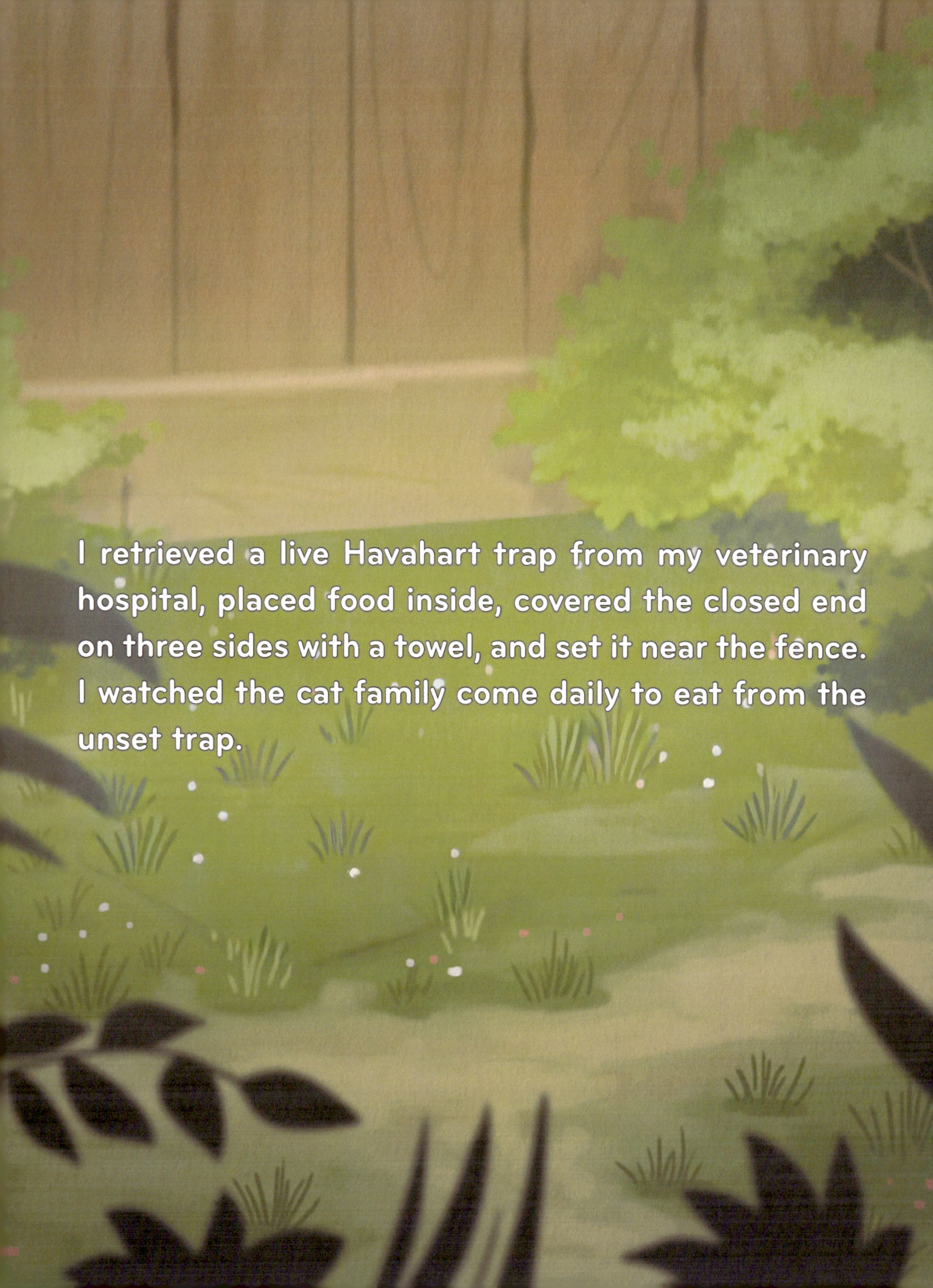

I retrieved a live Havahart trap from my veterinary hospital, placed food inside, covered the closed end on three sides with a towel, and set it near the fence. I watched the cat family come daily to eat from the unset trap.

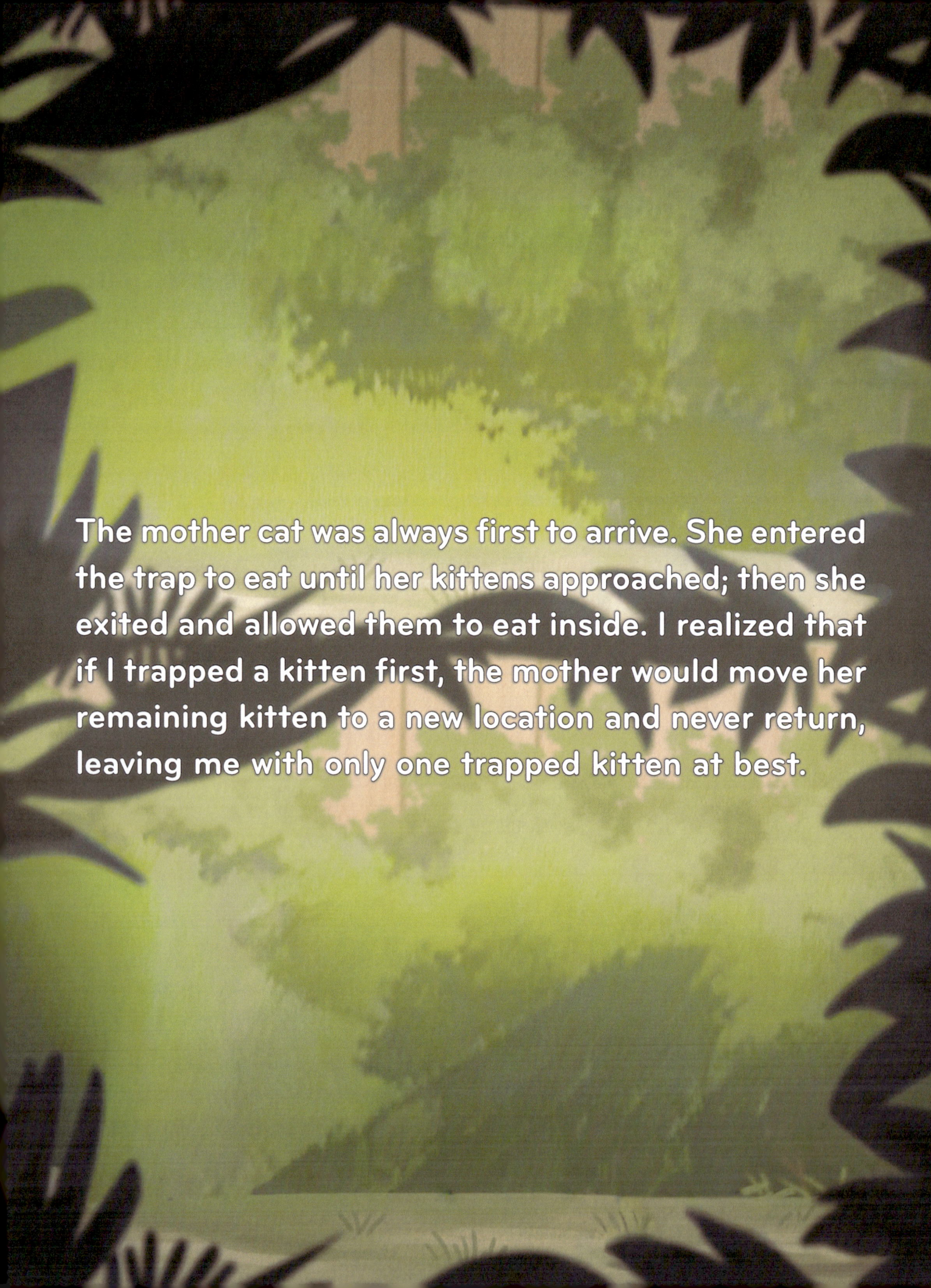

The mother cat was always first to arrive. She entered the trap to eat until her kittens approached; then she exited and allowed them to eat inside. I realized that if I trapped a kitten first, the mother would move her remaining kitten to a new location and never return, leaving me with only one trapped kitten at best.

After several days, the mother was no longer hesitant to enter the trap. On 09/20/2001, right on schedule, she walked inside, and the trap door shut behind her. I took her to Camden Pet Hospital, and she proved to be truly wild. We placed the trap inside a large black plastic yard bag and pumped gas anesthetic and oxygen through a tube until she was sleepy enough for us to place an endotracheal tube and maintain anesthesia. While she slept, we performed a physical exam, bathed her, treated her for fleas, spayed her, administered vaccines, and placed her in an observation cage.

After two weeks with no progress toward taming her, I gave up and returned her home in the same trap. I released her, continued to leave food for her, and she typically came to eat before slipping under the front gate and disappearing across the street. I never again saw her return to the tin shed.

As for the kittens, I trapped one on September 21 and the other on September 22. To encourage bonding with humans, we isolated them from each other. Alone, with only friendly people and good food around, they quickly became socialized and were adopted into new homes. One went to our receptionist, Nancy Itri. His name was Sammy. He passed away before Momma Cat, on January 29, 2017. The father cat was a large, battle-scarred white tom. During mating season, he and other males could be heard fighting through the night. My hospital note read, "He has no routine, and I will never catch him." And that was the truth.

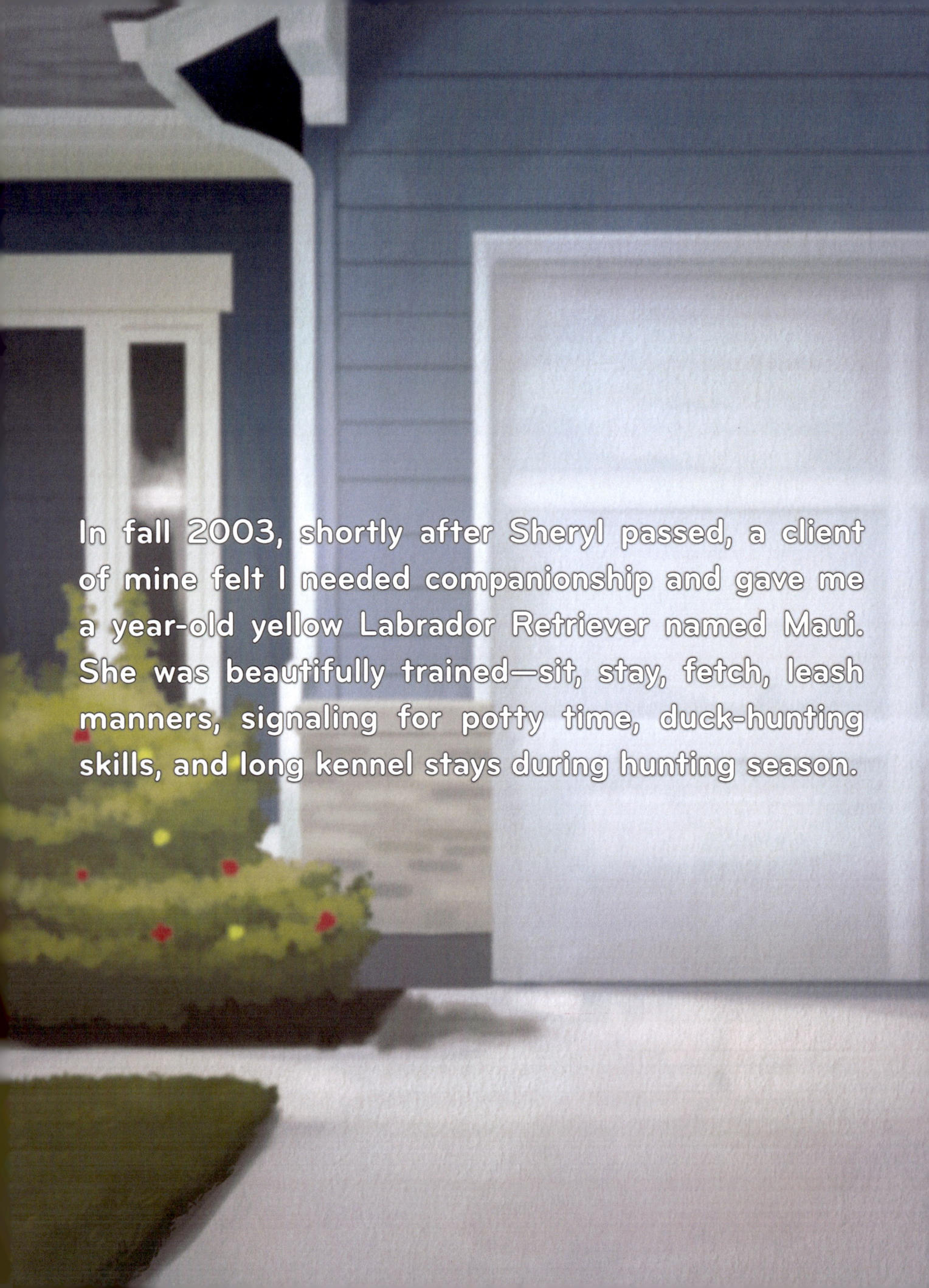

In fall 2003, shortly after Sheryl passed, a client of mine felt I needed companionship and gave me a year-old yellow Labrador Retriever named Maui. She was beautifully trained—sit, stay, fetch, leash manners, signaling for potty time, duck-hunting skills, and long kennel stays during hunting season.

She didn't get along well with the client's other dogs, but I enjoyed her immensely. I'll never forget her first night with me. Not knowing what to expect, I didn't want her in the yard or loose in the house, so I kept her tied on a leash to the bed's headboard. During the night, I heard licking sounds and discovered she had chewed a hole in the carpet beneath the bed. The client explained she was used to sleeping in a crate during hunting season.

The next night, I placed a kennel in my bedroom and told her to "kennel." She obeyed, and we both slept well. Her new routine became: morning potty break, breakfast, often a ride to work—illegally sitting beside me in the car—and time in the backyard while I worked. At night it was "Kennel, Maui," and I'd close the door of the crate in my bedroom for most of her life.

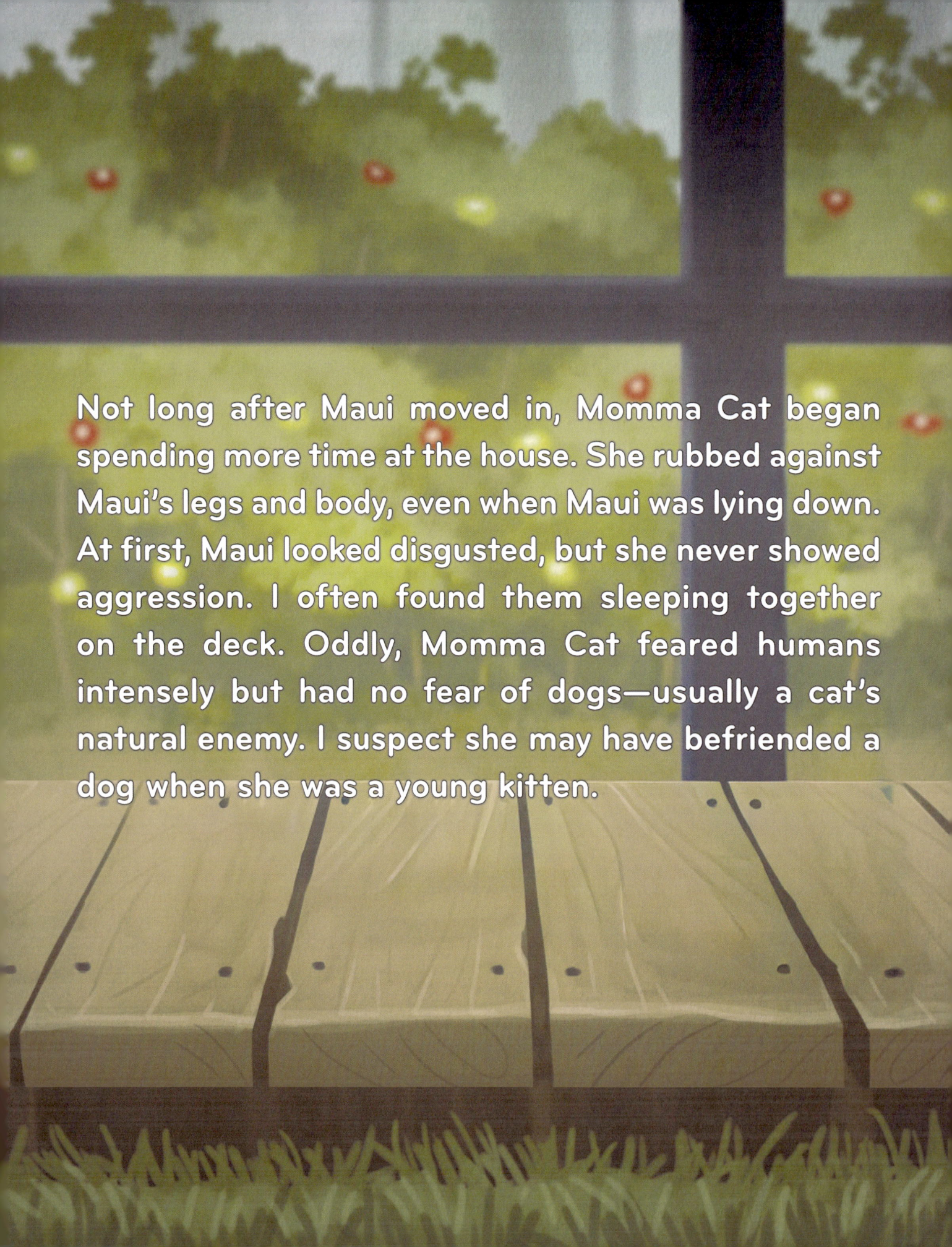

Not long after Maui moved in, Momma Cat began spending more time at the house. She rubbed against Maui's legs and body, even when Maui was lying down. At first, Maui looked disgusted, but she never showed aggression. I often found them sleeping together on the deck. Oddly, Momma Cat feared humans intensely but had no fear of dogs—usually a cat's natural enemy. I suspect she may have befriended a dog when she was a young kitten.

With patience during feeding, Momma Cat eventually rubbed against my legs. If I sat in a chair with my arms hanging down, she would rub her back beneath my hands. At times, I could rub her ears or gently hold the base of her tail as she pulled it slowly away.

Fourteen years later, Maui began developing age-related health problems, including potty accidents. She eventually spent most of her time at Camden Pet Hospital, where she could receive proper care. She passed on March 10, 2017.

Momma Cat continued staying around the house during the day, mostly on the backyard deck. As years passed, she slept more, and I could approach her without waking her. Concerned about her hearing loss, cloudy eyes, and the risk of being hit by a car or attacked, I borrowed the Havahart trap again. She was wary and entered only when I sat nearby. Even then, she stayed quick enough to avoid triggering the trap. Eventually, I held the trap door open with one hand, partially blocked the exit with the other, and dropped the door manually. It worked—though she still put up quite a fight.

I brought her back to Camden Pet Hospital, where her "fairy godmother" and the staff helped transform her into a completely different cat than the one I had known. They bathed and brushed her, ran lab tests, cuddled her, fed her pieces of their lunches, and helped her overcome her fear of humans. She lived freely in the break room and was never caged again.

She was nearly blind, likely seeing only shadows. Her hearing was minimal. Her heart was enlarged with a loud murmur, her kidneys were small and failing, her remaining teeth were infected, and she was painfully thin. Records showed hyperthyroidism, heart and kidney failure, and chronic severe arthritis. By all accounts, it was a miracle she was still alive. Feline hyperthyroidism is common in older cats and caused by benign thyroid tumors producing excess hormones, accelerating metabolism. Symptoms include weight loss despite increased appetite, increased thirst and urination, hyperactivity, vomiting, and diarrhea.

For me, those days at work were precious. I watched her emerge from her sleeping area without fear of humans, limping slowly toward me to sniff a treat or piece of my lunch. She allowed us to pick her up and gently pet her. At long last, I had become one of her trusted friends.

Momma Cat stayed at the hospital 24/7 for several months, taking her medications as she gradually grew thinner and weaker. One day she didn't come out of her hiding spot. She seemed unconscious and was breathing very slowly. The staff gathered around. I told her I loved her and how important she had been in my life as I gently gave her an injection to help her return to the Maker of us all. Since then, whenever I hear a cooing dove or see one in flight, I think of Momma Cat and her kittens, calling out peace and hope to the world—just as the Bible describes.

I have the urns of Maui (dated March 2017) and Momma Cat (dated October 2018), each with a paw print and picture. Momma Cat's urn rests atop Maui's. Someday I'll be placed in a box as well. Knowing my family, it will be viewed briefly and then buried. Perhaps—before they close my box—someone will place Maui's urn in my left hand and Momma Cat's in my right, and have their names engraved on my headstone.